Wounded *but* Healed

LaVinia Young

Kingdom Builders Publications LLC

© 2018 Lavinia B. Young
Kingdom Builders Publications

All rights reserved. No part of this book may be reproduced or transmitted in any form or by any means without written permission from the author.

Printed in the USA
SOFT COVER ISBN 9780578139913
Library of Congress Control Number **2018950356**

All Scriptures used by King James Version with the exception of one text from the Amplified Version

Authored by LaVinia Young

Edited by Lakisha S. Forrester
Kingdom Builders Publications

Photographer
Portraits Innovations

Cover Design
LoMar Designs

Contact information:
Oasis of Hope
oasisofhopeoutreach@aol.com
kbpublications@sc.rr.com

This Book Belongs to

DEDICATION

I dedicate this book to my mother, the late Pastor Martha Young. Without her prayers and encouragements, this book wouldn't have been possible.

Also, to my late husband, Luke Albert Brown, who always said, "*Never let anyone stop you from doing what God called you to do, not even me!*"

This book is a by-product of his encouragement to never quit.

CONTENTS

	Dedication	iv
	Introduction	1
1	The Miracle Surrounding my Birth	4
2	My Hurt	12
3	Why God?	22
4	Satan's Plot	35
5	Don't Blame God	50
6	Pastor's Abandonment	56
7	Revealing a Pastor's Heart	61
8	Mastering Your Emotions	67
9	Freedom through Forgiveness	71
10	My Resurrection	80
11	You are an Overcomer	84
12	Repairer of the Breach	89
	A Prayer for You	92
	Acknowledgments	94
	About the Author	95

INTRODUCTION

We have three enemies – the world, the flesh, and the devil. This work is designed to expose the culprits, Satan, and his demons. Those evil forces are responsible for hurts on many levels. People tend to blame God, but God is for His work. He is not the author of confusion or strife. Where envy and strife are, there is confusion and every evil work. Church hurt is just one way Satan plots to distract you from your destiny.

Moses was a prime example. He saw an Egyptian slave master beating a Hebrew slave, one of his own kind. So, he killed him. The next day, Moses was confronted, fear gripped him, and he ran away into the desert. He spent forty years in the wilderness. Satan caused him to run from God instead of to God. God will never leave you, but you can leave Him. In the end, you still must answer the call. God is so loving and caring. In the desert, He used a burning bush to get Moses' attention. If Moses had not taken the time to turn toward the burning bush, his end would have been different. But, thank God, he did. It is important to remember that God will not force you to do anything. He has given each of us free will. In your place of wilderness, God will be there for you the way He was there for Moses if you let Him. Satan may have driven you there, but if you seek God, He will show you the way out. Even Jesus was led into the wilderness to be tempted by the devil. However, He overcame Satan, because He used the Word to defeat him.

When we are in the wilderness, despondent, hurt, and feel there is no way out, we tend to have a pity party. However, this is not the attitude of a winner. God expects us to stand. But, our flesh wants nothing to do with God. Therefore, we need to embrace His Word, if we are going to win. We must overcome our hurts by the blood of the Lamb and the word of our testimony (*Revelation 12:11*). The pain goes deep because we put so much emphasis on the fact that God can do anything. We may ponder and question why God did not stop the hurt, since this is His church. We must realize that we live in a fallen world where Satan is god of this world; and he gets joy out of using and working through believers. Humanity are fallen beings, and as they yield, they give Satan access to their life. The scripture says, "We wrestle not against flesh and blood, but the spirit behind the person, principalities, powers, rulers of the darkness of this world, and wicked spirits in the heavenly places" (*Ephesians 6:12*). Satan's evil, well-organized plan is to bring destruction against the Body of Christ.

My prayer is that this book will be an answer guide to hurts you have experienced, and that you read it prayerfully with an open mind and heart. God is waiting to flood your heart with the light of His loving grace; thereby, setting you free from the bondage of Satan. Whom the Son has set free is free indeed. As you receive revelation, stand fast in the liberty where Christ has made you free.

•·········•

THE MIRACLE SURROUNDING MY BIRTH
Chapter 1

While in the womb, Jesus allowed me to take shape. Satan and his demons had an assignment to bring such hardships and destruction that would lead me to aborting the plan and purpose God laid out for my life. Scripture says, we overcome by the blood of the Lamb and the words of our testimony *(Revelation 12:11)*. When his plans failed with my birth, he went to another level. This chapter is my testimony about the Child, the Miracle, and the Revelation.

The Child

Satan attacks in the infancy stage of any dream or vision. There was great warfare against my purpose, at the early stages of my life. Once I left my mother's womb, it was not long before a spirit of fear bound me. I could not go to sleep without having lights on in the entire house. At 11 months, my cousin and I were playing around a very hot pot-belly wood stove. In the 1950s, my parents used that stove to cook and warm the house. My cousin pushed me on the stove. When they pulled me from the stove, the whole left side of my face had third degree burns. Looking at me today, in my sixties, you would never know I experienced such trauma. Satan's plan to disfigure my face did not work. I needed not one ounce of plastic surgery. To God Be the Glory!

I was also an introverted child. I found it difficult to talk to anyone, unless it was only one person in a room. Even with that one person, there were certain conditions that had to be met before I would speak: the lights had to be out, and the doors had to be locked. I also had a speech impediment. In school, I attended speech labs, but nothing worked. After receiving salvation, the Holy Spirit released my tongue. So, Satan's plan to thwart the plan of God for me to spread the gospel, teach, and preach were overthrown. His plan to tie my tongue did not work.

I was always aware of a presence, when I was growing up. I did not know what to call that presence, so I started referring to it as "my friend." I grew up in a large family. I am the fifth of fourteen children. There was never a quiet moment around our house. I knew if I was going to hear what my friend wanted to say, I would have to find a quiet place to listen. I would find those places under the bed or in the closet. Sometimes, I would fall asleep for hours in my quiet, hiding places. One time, my family even had to form a neighborhood search party to find me.

I vividly remember sitting in a homemade swing in our backyard, wondering what, or who was beyond the clouds. I did know that Jesus was on the other side. I thought if I swung high enough, I possibly could reach Him. There was always something special about my friend. I felt a love and a connection that I could not explain to anyone. Now, I know it was, and still is, the Spirit of God.

As I grew, the experiences became stronger and more real to me. Between the ages of five and six, when I would retire for the night, before my head hit the pillow, I felt myself drifting into outer space. I felt like I was in an atmosphere in the sky, above the stars. During those times, strange noises would flow from my belly and out of my mouth. I was always afraid that those noises were going to wake up my siblings, since we lived in a crowded space. We only had two bedrooms. Therefore, we had to sleep six to a bed, three at each end. As the family continued to grow, my parents had to add another bed inside their room. Then, we had to add another bed in our room, when my adult cousin came to live with us.

After receiving the Baptism of the Holy Spirit as an adult, Jesus explained to me that what I was experiencing as a child was me praying in the Spirit and that those prayers were still being answered. As a young girl, as those sounds continued to flow, Satan told me that I was mentally challenged. He convinced me that if I told anyone, I would be committed to the mental hospital. At the time, I did not know it was a lie and I did not know it was Satan. I believed those thoughts in my head. In other words, I believed Satan. So, therefore, I kept it a secret until I was an adult.

Because of my childhood experiences, I was always interested in the supernatural realm. At the age of 18, I accompanied a loved one, who was experiencing satanic sickness, to a witch doctor. During this entire visit, the witch doctor's eyes and attention were fixated on me. At the end of this visit, he approached me, along with my loved one, and began speaking over my life and laying hands on me. At the time, I was eight months pregnant. I felt my child kick in the womb, which caused me almost to hit the floor. I did not know it then, but he released a satanic power into my life. Shortly after, I began to experience unusual powers. I began to have astral projections, or out-of-body experiences. I felt as if I had no control over my life. I gave birth one month later to a son. For nine years, my son suffered from satanic oppression and tormenting spirits mainly at night. There were many hospital visits with no explanation for his suffering.

God explained to me that Satan used me in my old life to pronounce curses and that now because of the power that's invested in me, through the Name of Jesus, whenever I pronounce a blessing, it shall be. Satan needed a body to work through, and I yielded because of my ignorance. The word ignorance is not meant to sound ugly. It simply means that you have no knowledge of a thing. But, when light comes, you must no longer walk in darkness. If you still choose to do just that, your darkness will become even darker. There are many yielding to Satan through occults, horror movies, certain music, etc. I could go on and on. Satan used all those things in his devised and deceptive plan to stop God's plan from coming to pass in my life.

The Miracle

In 1954, Mom found out she was expecting. At the time, she already had two boys and two girls. Well-meaning people told her to abort the child. But, she decided to tune anyone out who spoke of abortion and go forth with her pregnancy. Five months into her pregnancy, she started experiencing complications. She visited her doctor, and the results showed she had a swollen appendix, as well as a tumor smothering her unborn child. The doctor told her he needed to do an emergency surgery, which could involve abortion or her own demise. She needed to think about it, because they did not have a lot of time. What pressure! But Mom was a woman of faith and prayer. She went home and talked to God. As she laid on her bed, Jesus appeared in the doorway of her bedroom. She said His voice was like the sound of thunder. Immediately, I had an unsettling in my spirit when she referred to His voice. Somehow, I knew what He said to her had to do with the child. All Mom remembered was laying her head on the pillow with doctors surrounding her bed, as Jesus led the operation. The next morning, she woke up and turned over slowly, saying she needed to be careful not to break the stitches. She returned to the doctor, and he could not explain what happened, except it had to be a miracle. What a mighty God we serve!

The Revelation

The unrest I had about His thunderous voice was there for a reason. I really needed my own revelation about my mother's miracle. The Holy Spirit told me to ask my mom to give her account again. He asked me to pray in the spirit. Because the Holy Spirit knows all things, He knows how to get the perfect will of God concerning the matter. I did as the Holy Spirit asked me to and prayed in tongues. He revealed the parts of the miracle that Mom did not have knowledge of. He told me that the doctors that Mom spoke of were not doctors in the natural. He said He came on her faith level, so she could believe. They were actually angelic beings. The voice of thunder was a heavenly language that directed the beings, so the child could live and not die.

Because He is a God of purpose, He does nothing without a purpose. The Holy Spirit told me that because that tumor tried to destroy me, the gifts of healing would flow through me. He said I will lay hands on thousands upon thousands, and they shall be healed. I saw evidence of this gift, when I ministered to a woman who suffered with fibroid tumors. I cursed those tumors at the roots. That woman later had X-rays. The results showed that one tumor was now brown and dried up, whereas, the others were still alive. Her doctors had no explanation for this. She later had surgery to address the other tumors.

God has designed us for a purpose. Our purpose proceeds our creation. I realize I have nothing to do with how God designed me. I am what I am by the grace of God. God also has a plan for your life. Satan has an assignment against your life. Do not allow his attacks against you to stop you from fulfilling your destiny. The doctors did not have the final say so for my life or my mother's. She is 87 years young and is a mighty woman of God. She continues to believe God's Word today with her appendix still intact.

Satan's attack in my womb did not work either. By the blood and the power of the name of Jesus, my son and I were both set free. All three of us have been walking with the Lord a long time. For my son it has been 35 years, and for me, 44 years. Of course, Mom has been walking much longer than that. To God be the glory!

MY HURT
Chapter 2

Because Satan was unable to bring my physical body under his rule, his next plan was to attack me in the place where I went to unite with other brothers and sisters. The place where I went to draw strength. The place where I went to learn the will of God for my life. Yes, Satan decided to attack me in the church. It was in that place, where I became broken, injured, wounded, and sustained an unimaginable amount of hurt and pain.

Let me give you a little background about my experiences with church. My mother, a Pentecostal Pastor, has always been a praying woman. In our youth, she held Bible Studies in our home once a week. We attended church every Sunday morning. Making excuses for not attending was not an option. Everything in our house that had breath had to be in church. I believe it was because Mom deposited the things of God in me at an early age, that my spirit became strong.

I always knew God had a plan and purpose for my life but did not know the road I had to tread to get there. I connected with a ministry and served faithfully for 31 years. My philosophy was, and still is, to serve God, my Father from my heart regardless of anything that happens. It was important to make sure that anything I did in the ministry would be done from my heart to the glory of God. Over those 31 years, I had the opportunity to serve in various auxiliaries, such as, a trustee with keys to the church, a janitor, a prayer leader, a New Convert Counselor, a Prayer Room Director, and a greeter. I also served in the Altar ministry and in the follow-up ministry. I traveled a total of four hours to and from our sister church to lead intercessory prayer, serve as an usher, and serve as the choir, praise, and worship leader. For 16 years, I served as the Prison/Jail Director. I served in every auxiliary, except the sound and nursery departments. Essentially, my home was where the Pastor, the First Lady, and his entourage stayed, when they traveled to my city. Providing meals, at my expense, and running errands were part of my service to them. I am not boasting about my works; I just want you to know how deeply I was involved in that ministry. I believe it was in part due to my mother's teaching that we should always serve and give honor and respect to men and women of God.

The ministry where I served was not one where the Pastor laid hands and sent members out to start their own work in the Lord. I believed that the foundation I laid in that ministry was going to be instrumental, because God was going to give me people just like myself. In my mid-50s, I began to wonder about the vision God placed in my heart about starting a ministry. I thought about how much time had passed since joining the ministry at age 32. Although I did not want to seem like I was rushing God, I certainly thought to myself that I was not getting any younger. I was becoming desperate for directions for the next level in my life.

Serving was my element. It brought me a great deal of joy. I even served as a caregiver, before retiring. I have always worked diligently. I did not work that way for a ministerial title, but to learn and grow. I believed that when God released me into ministry, I would have the experience I needed to nurture the people. I also believed that God would give me the kind of members that would be like me. It was important for me to do things with integrity and in the spirit of excellence.

At the age of 55, I realized that I was not going to be released by my Pastor to pursue those works in the Lord. Through prayer, the Word, prophecy, and the witness of the Spirit, I began seeking God fervently for His directions. God began to prepare me for Bible College. When I felt I had the confirmation I needed from the Lord, I went to my Pastor with a clear plan and was hoping to receive his input and blessing. Instead of the outcome I was expecting, I was shot down, yelled at, and felt intimidated. "That didn't come from God, but from your mind," he alluded.

That really did hurt! Those words really stung me. I knew that I heard from God. But, what do you do in a situation like this? I thought to myself, "Wow, I was a leader who wore seven hats in the church. I even sat on the front row." But, according to the Pastor, I was not a recognized minister. I honestly started to look around and began comparing myself to others. Some members spent nearly forty years and were never licensed to be ministers. Others spent less time and performed lesser works than I did in the ministry; and they became licensed. I will not deny that this was a confusing time in my life. I knew that regardless, I had to keep seeking God and thanking Him, despite the circumstances. I had to stay focused.

I began to see confusion erupt in the house of God. Before Bible Study on Wednesday nights, there was typically a question and answer session. There was a young woman who asked a question that started with the words, "Minister Young." The Pastor stopped her in mid-sentence with a simple question, "Who is Minister Young?" A puzzled look ran across her face as if she did something wrong. I thought, "Wow, all of this because I wanted to leave to progress in the things of God and attend Bible College!"

After I officially announced that I was leaving, I sat on the front row for one year and listened to what I felt were innuendos thrown from the pulpit about me. It was abundantly clear as I listened to his preaching that he was very angry with me. To me, this made no sense. Suddenly, it seemed as if the quality of my work was now being challenged. In all those years, he never once questioned or presented any dissatisfaction regarding my work. I felt like my character came under attack. I believe this was done solely to cause a stain on my name. Because I looked to him as a father for the last 31 years, I surely was disappointed. I started to feel like no matter what I needed to do for my own life, I was met with opposition from the Pastor. When my secular job wanted me to relocate for seven weeks to work on a project, he was concerned about who was going to cover the auxiliaries I oversaw. At this point, now more than ever I was determined to follow the leading of God.

I had planned to return to the ministry after my two years in Bible College, but because of his cruel treatment, I knew there was no way I could have continued to sit under his leadership. About four months before leaving, during a leadership meeting, I made sure that I spoke with the person over all auxiliaries. I wanted to make sure that the leader knew my ending date so there would be adequate time to find replacements for me. In addition, I made sure our sister church was on the same page, because I wanted to make sure nothing was left lacking. I felt that was necessary because I wanted to continue to demonstrate integrity.

For eight months, I eagerly awaited his response. But, it did not come as I expected. I imagine that once he shot the idea down in his mind, there was no need to address it publicly or privately. I decided to mention it again one night after Bible Study. I reminded him that the upcoming Sunday would be my last Sunday. He looked at me and shrugged his shoulders. It felt very dismissive. On Sundays, at the end of service, there was usually a line of congregants waiting to speak with him. I figured I should get in line also. He merely looked at me and walked away. His personal assistant immediately told me that the line was closed.

This event really did cause me to be angry. I desperately felt that I needed to cross paths with him. I needed our eyes to meet, so we can discuss me leaving. When we did get face-to-face, he pointed his finger in my face and began to chastise me. I felt like a five-year-old at that moment. As he shook his pointed finger in my face, he said, "If you had done it right, it would have been differently." But, this was not done in private and quietly. It was almost as if he wanted the audience of onlookers to hear him. He continued to say, "I want it to be known to all that I am not sending you out, and by the way, you did not do it right." As he walked away, he told me to keep in touch.

I was not exactly looking for a going away party. After 31 years, I would like to have some mentioning of me leaving. Of course, some of the members knew, because I told them I was going to attend Bible College. Although I was hurt, I had to make sure that I maintained my integrity. When your spirit becomes weak and broken, sometimes it feels like it is hard to rise. I wanted God to count me as faithful. I realized that being honest and having strong morals and principles were important. I made sure that regardless of the hurt, I was not going to practice manipulation by trying to get others to turn against the Pastor because of what was happening to me. I did not want any blockages in my heart to hinder me physically or spiritually. Whatever God had for me, I wanted to receive it in spirit and in truth.

Because of this hurt, this nightmare, this painful experience, I began to put up walls of defense around my heart and my life. That was the exact moment when things began going downhill for me. I prayed, and the Lord showed me that I was operating in self-centeredness and pride. I desired God's blessings, so I began to work on every negative aspect that overshadowed who I was to be in Christ. I was not just looking for God to bless me materially, but my ultimate desire was spiritual maturity. I realized that my words and actions were important, if I was going to walk in victory. I practiced a lot of self-talk. I prayed a lot and kept trying to remember that my character is who I was inwardly. The Spirit would remind me that the Pastor was trying to make me out of something that I was not.

That was the moment I found out that my character was being attacked. Even after the fact, it seemed like 90% of the people in church were instructed not to associate with me. I felt abandoned for sure. I spent the last 31 years a part of what I thought was my church family. According to the Pastor, I did not leave with his blessing, and they were forbidden from speaking with me because of a scripture that was taken out of context. *1 Corinthians 5:11* was quoted to the congregation about me. They were told not to even sit at the table or even eat with me. However, that scripture really referred to the fornicators, the covetousness, idolaters, railers, drunkards, and the extortioners.

God showed me in a dream of how angry the Pastor was. In that dream, the Pastor used a lot of profanity. It was then that I realized that his anger for me was not about building the kingdom of God, but because he was losing a good worker. It was then that I knew I overcame and I had the victory. I did know the truth of who I was. I decided to stand on that truth. Of course, I was concerned about my reputation. That was mainly because, in my opinion, I felt that a scarred reputation would cause people not to hear you and cause you to lose influence within the Body of Christ. The strength of my character prevailed, because I was doing the work on myself that was needed. I knew I had to protect myself by protecting my mind, and not allowing anyone to cause me to go against my convictions. If I did, I felt I would eventually regret it. I began to call Satan out for who he was, is, and always will be, and that was a LIAR!

WHY GOD?
Chapter 3

One of my favorite passages in the Old Testament is **Psalms 42:11**. *"Why art thou cast down oh my soul...hope thou in God."* Another is **Proverbs 51:17** that says, *"A broken and contrite spirit he will not despise."* These scriptures exemplify why Satan schemes and devises plots to destroy the spirit of humanity. This is how he attempts to get us to turn from the Father. Satan could care less about our family, our finances, or us. His number one goal is to make sure that grief occurs. He wants our Father in heaven to grieve for us. He also wants us to grieve.

I believe Satan uses hurts and offenses in the church to cause damage to the believer and to prevent the nonbeliever from becoming believers. Church hurt affects the spirit of man, because in our minds, church should be a haven, a place of refuge and security. Why? Well, when we think of church, we think of a good God who is watching and protecting His flock. After all, what could possibly go wrong when we are in His house...right? I believe in my case, Satan used the hurt I experienced in church to stop God's plan for me. Has Satan caused you to stumble in the house of worship because of his tactics? I am sure there are many instances that have occurred, if not in your own lives, but perhaps, in the lives of others.

Satan does not always strike at the church within the walls of a private community. Sometimes, he wants to make national news. This was evident on the evening of June 17, 2015; a young, very disturbed man went into a church in Charleston, South Carolina, pretending to be a part of the Bible Study. He yielded to the enemy of his mind and carried out Satan's plan of such a horrendous act of murdering the Pastor and eight of his parishioners. I am sure many of us thought to ourselves or even vocalized, "Why God? Why didn't you protect them?" Yes, it happened in the house of God, and those individuals were born again believers. God said with long life, would He satisfy us and show us His salvation. Please, know that this was Satan's doing. The individual who committed this horrible crime sowed a seed of death. He has been sentenced to death. He was a tool used in Satan's plan concerning God's precious children who are now with Him in Heaven.

We cannot lose sight that we are in a fallen world. Satan is the god (small g) of this world. He is a thief who comes to steal, kill, and destroy. The kingdom of God operates through kingdom principles and spiritual laws. Let us put the blame on Satan and not Father God. Yes, God is all-powerful. But, He will never go against the laws He has established. I wonder if this hurt has caused any to turn from Father God. It is my prayer that everyone will understand the true nature of God and realize that His tender mercies are over all His works.

Just as the Holy Spirit needs a body to work through, Satan also needs a body to work through. We must make a choice to yield and be used by either one of them. I say choose God. We are in a fallen world where demon forces are present to bring destruction to mankind. Satan is walking about, as a roaring lion, seeking whom he may devour. If he had the ability to destroy all Christians at will, why hasn't he done it already? It is because he only has power to those who yield. Sin shall not have dominion over the children of God, who have confessed, repented, and turned from their wicked ways. God made humanity as beings with the freedom of choice to do as they will. However, we must choose wisely.

The only thing that can stop God from working in our lives is our own wills. He will never override the will of man.

God has put before us, life and death, blessings, and curses. He tells us to choose life. We need to water the seed of righteousness to live. Even though His tender mercies are over all His works, if you choose death, you set a spiritual law against your life. Because of the law of seeding, harvests must come to pass with time. If you plant and sow good seeds, you will reap a good harvest. To do the opposite will result in a bad harvest.

Anytime you experience hurt of any kind, keep in mind, it is never from God because He builds up His Church. He does not do so to tear it down causing division and discord. No, that is Satan's satanic job. **Proverbs 6:16-19** says, *there are six things God hates, seven is an abomination to Him; one who sows discord among the brethren.* God is not the author of confusion, but a God of peace. Anytime you begin to experience strife and confusion, watch out, because Satan is on the rampage, seeking anyone who will yield, so that his will can be accomplished. Never engage in backbiting or gossiping, because eventually, it will cost you. In some cases, it could cost you a price you cannot pay. We must keep in mind, who our enemies are – the world, the flesh, and the devil. God is good. Satan is bad. God came that we might have an abundant life. Anything outside of an abundant life in faith is not the character of God, but of Satan's.

Being wounded in church is a plot designed by Satan to destroy mankind, thereby, grieving the heart of the Father. Satan gets joy out of using Christians, or should I say, born again believers. It is important to note that Christians should exemplify Christ-like character. Some hurts you experience from born again believers are not Christ-like, but is from the flesh, simply because they have not renewed their minds to the Word of God. Satan's ultimate plan is to break our spirit, thereby, causing us to walk away from God and our local assembly. He tries to lure us away from the body of believers to make us a lone wolf, a person who prefers to act or be alone. BINGO! He has you where he wants you…trapped. He knows the power of unity. There is strength in unity, because this is where God commands the blessings. One can put a thousand to flight; two can put ten thousand to flight. Even though **Psalm 133:1** says, *how good and pleasant it is for brethren to dwell together in unity*, if believers don't see the importance of this command and practice it, they give Satan access not only in their life, but also in their local assembly.

I saw a statistic once that said 70% of professing Christians of faith do not attend church because of being hurt there. I am sure this grieves the heart of the Father. My prayer is that we should all take part, in some form of fashion, of reaching the 70%, so that we can show them who God really is. Who is God? God is a yoke destroyer, a mind regulator, a burden lifter, and the author and finisher of our faith. We are instructed not to forsake the assembling of ourselves as we see the time drawing near. Satan's job is to bring disillusionment to the Body of Christ. He makes the hurting believers believe that Christianity is not as good as they believe it to be. He makes the nonbelievers not even want to try Jesus. Many people buy his lies. Let us refuse to buy his lies. Let us spread the good news of the gospel to anyone we encounter. *Jude 1:24* says, that *God is the one that can keep us from falling and present us faultless before his presence*. What an awesome God we serve!

Offenses will come which is a part of this Christian walk. We all may have to walk in the valley or live in the wilderness for a period of time. It is inevitable, because God uses those experiences to grow and mature us in Him. We must enroll in the "school of *knee*-ology." That means we need to get and stay on our knees in prayer. Jesus was led into the wilderness by the Spirit to be tempted forty days. Our flesh makes some of us want to give up and quit after forty minutes. From time to time, life will throw us daggers. We all have a choice to take it and cut our way out or allow those daggers to stay in our hearts and cause us to bleed to death in the spirit. We never know who God has on the other side of our trials to minister to once we come out of them. "Wow that really was for my good, Lord! Now I see why I went through it; it was to help someone else!" Have you ever said those statements to yourself while you are going through? Most of us have not. We tend to see the benefit of our tests, once we have declared them to be testimonies.

I know it may be hard sometimes to rejoice when we are hurting. But, we must do it. We are required to thank God in all things. Perhaps, seeking wise counsel can help us learn to do just that. We may need to surround ourselves with men and women of God who are overcomers and seekers of God's heart. We should even pray about who God would want us to commune with in this season. Essentially, we are to pray about everything. Christians are not meant to be weak. If you know you are sensing His leading, run to Him. In **Hosea 11:10**, *God will roar like a mighty lion inviting all of His children to come*. Let us listen for the roar of God and not the one of Satan's. If we listen to Satan's roar, we will be AMBUSHED!

We should not second-guess what we know God is saying. We cannot let man's opinion of us dictate who we are or cause us to override our convictions in Christ Jesus. We must seek God. The Holy Spirit will lead us. We should always respect the office our leader holds, and trust that God will reveal what He needs to reveal if he or she is in error. We should take the gavel out of our hands, because God is the ultimate judge. Do you remember when God showed Moses the Promised Land for the people? Wasn't that magnificent? But, Moses was not the one to take them in. Our leader is part of the plan to get us from one level to another. Some leaders will take us as far as they can, but God is the one who will direct us to the next level. Always keep an open mind and heart to hear His leading. You are simply the vehicle God is using to carry out His plan in the Earth.

Sometimes, people will think that we have lost our minds, when God has us to step out on faith. When God instructed me to move to Colorado Springs for two years to attend Bible College, my family thought I lost my mind. That probably was because I drove in pain from the surgery, rather than take a flight. I will never forget those two and a half days of driving. I remember when the sun went down, I checked into a hotel. When it rose at dawn, I checked out of the hotel, and started my cross-country journey. I barely listened to the music I had in my CD player. In fact, within 24 hours, I think I only listened to it twice. I spent most of my ordained trip having Father-Daughter time. What a life-changing trip and the best decision of obedience ever!

If you are thinking about ministry, take my advice. Never force ministry. Do not just get up one day and say, "Oh, I think I am called to preach and I am going to start my own ministry." Christ should lead us. We should never do anything out of vain conceit and glory for ourselves. We do not want to discredit the name of Jesus by walking in a calling that He did not assign to us. There are times in faith when people may discredit us. Of course, we are all entitled to own opinions. I like how our mighty God does things. If it is of Him, He will show and prove to the naysayers. Therefore, we have to keep going because there are people out there that God has assigned for us to reach. We cannot effectively reach them holding on to past hurts. We should never aim to be the people talking about the Word of God with angry and bothersome looks on our faces. We should draw people in with the light of Christ. They should be able to see the glory of God on us, and not be turned off by an angry disposition.

No matter how bad we have been hurt, it will not and cannot compare to the ridicule, shaming, and violence that Jesus experienced for us! He told us in ***John 15:20*** that *we would endure persecution,* because He endured persecution. He experienced that persecution just for us! What an awesome ruler and protector! We should be joyful, because He lived, therefore, we shall live. Jesus stayed focused, even while receiving those lashes and being nailed to a cross. When we break focus, it can become a detriment to our lives. We do not want to hinder the lives of others that the Father has assigned for us to spread the good news to. Look at the fruit of His life today. We have that same fruit also, if we just operate in it consistently. What a wonderful Christ who supplies us with tender mercies and grace!

Many believers, who have experienced hurt in their local assemblies, have written off the entire Body of Christ. We should always pray for discernment in a matter. If we do not, *we are subject to being weak, sick, and even dying*, as *1 Corinthians 11:30* states. Imagine being so busy at your duties, and you suddenly bite your tongue for no reason. Would you pull out all your teeth, because they hurt your tongue? Probably not...right? That sounds a bit foolish. But, it is also foolish, in a spiritual sense, to cut off the entire body because of a few bad apples. Perhaps, we may need to pray and ask God if we are to continue in a ministry under a particular leadership, or if He is releasing us to be fed elsewhere. Have you ever felt a disconnection within yourself, if you have separated from the Body of Christ for a certain time? It's probably because we were designed to be fitly joined together, being one in Christ. *1 Corinthians 12:21* says, *"The eye can't say to the hand I have no need of you." God's headship is exercised for the church* as is stated in *Ephesians 1:22*. Even if you may no longer fellowship at that local assembly, you are still in the body. It is important that we all work for the same purpose and that is to exercise Christ's authority through our bodies in the Earth. We need one another to fulfill God's plan in the Earth.

Do not get me wrong, I am not condoning broken fellowships. However, we do need to be careful about our feeding grounds. If there is a difference of opinion concerning doctrinal belief, and you can prove it through scripture, I believe you now have the right to disassociate yourself from that feeding ground. I am talking about doctrinal differences that are contrary to the Word of God. ***1 Corinthians 15:33*** tells us to *take heed to what you hear, because evil communication corrupts good manners.* According to ***1 Timothy 4:1****, there are doctrines of devils and if we are not careful, we will follow them.*

Perhaps, you have been ex-communicated from a church you loved and served for years. Or, maybe your leader may not agree with what you believe and know that God is leading you to do. Whatever the case, decide to walk in love and with the spirit of forgiveness. My leader did not agree and did not want to release me. Even though I knew what God was communicating to my heart, I still knew I needed my Pastor's blessings. I told him if he did not release me that

I would not go. He never said yes or no to my release, or that he did not think this was of God. I made the decision to trust and fear the Lord, rather than man, despite my hurts. Deep down I knew that I would have to give an account for the work God called me to do, as we all will. So, I toughened up, took the hard road, which was following God's plan. I said it was hard, because sometimes, we have to walk that road by ourselves with just Him for a while. I am so thankful that God knew the thoughts and intentions of my heart. It was hard, but I kept my heart right before God. What is your heart communicating to God? ***Jude 1:21*** says, *keep yourself in the love of God. Love never fails.*

SATAN'S PLOT
Chapter 4

Satan's plot is to destroy our lives. Satan walks about as a roaring lion seeking whom he may devour. If he had the power to devour at will; all Christians would be dead. We cannot give him that power. Satan is a defeated foe without power, because Jesus was manifested to destroy his works. We must remember that our lives are hidden with Christ in God. Christ is seated at the right hand of the Father making intercession for us, praying for us. It is in Him that we live, move, and have our being.

In the Garden of Gethsemane, Jesus prayed for those who were to believe on Him. He prayed to make them one, as He and the Father were one. Jesus prayed for Simon Peter that his faith would not fail. He was and is always praying for us; therefore, we are never alone. During the times when we may feel empty, alone, and full of sorrow, Jesus is waiting for us to call. Satan tries to oppress us, so we could give up on life and give up on God.

I can say that there are days when I wake up

and I do not feel saved. I thank Jesus that feelings have nothing to do with my salvation. Satan knows the joy of the Lord is our strength. Satan tries to steal our strength. Satan wants us to operate in weakness and succumb to despair so that he can take our joy. Let us remember that Satan has no power over a born-again believer, unless we give it to him. We have rights and privileges in Christ Jesus. No more should we let any lack of knowledge or fear rob us from the power of God. I thank God that the spirit of fear no longer binds me.

Yes, Satan attacks the Body of Christ through division and hurt. Yes, his goal is to stop God's plan from flowing through the Earth. If the Body of Christ does not operate in unity, the work of the Lord will be hindered. Let us examine some of Satan's little tactics that he uses to create big chaos. Imagine someone walking by without speaking to us. We may be hurt or offended if that occurs. But, that person simply may have had things on his or her mind and simply did not see us. Or, how about the tithing? Satan uses justifications by getting us to ask ourselves if we should be tithing because that was in the Old Testament, and we are living in the New Testament dispensation.

Satan is always fighting to keep us from going to church. He can create tension with husbands and wives, which causes arguments to occur on a Friday. Because of the offenses, by Sunday, they can be so angry at each other that the ride to the church is difficult. They cannot hear the Word in church. Then, they drive back home from church still in anger. It is important that we prepare our hearts to receive the implanted Word of God daily. The distractions that Satan assigns his demons to operate in churches are not new. However, we must be aware that he does scheme, and not give our seeds of righteousness over to him. Maybe we can even start preparing ourselves on the weekend to have our hearts and minds open to receiving Sunday's message. Of course, Saturdays are generally our day off from work, and we want to enjoy each one of them. We get to go to work on Mondays and brag about what we did on those fun Saturdays. If we spend all day Saturday engaging in activities and fail to put a little Word or prayer in on that day, we can possibly fall asleep during Sunday's message or even be too tired to go to church.

Five of Satan's Strongest Plots
- Sickness and Disease
- Unforgiveness
- Finances
- Family Unit
- Selfish Gratification

Sickness and Disease

Although we are called the Body of Christ, Satan tries to attack us with sickness. If he can weaken our bodies, we can become limited in expressing Jesus to the world. Perhaps, Satan has rationalized that we cannot read the Word if we are blind. Or, maybe we are unable to speak the Word if we are having problems with our vocal cords. Or, maybe we cannot lay hands on the sick if we, ourselves, have lost a limb. Those are just a few areas of our bodies that can come under attack. But, I say to you, we need to speak to our bodies and confess God's Word. When pain attacks your body, refuse to agree with the symptoms. Set a guard over your mouth, keep watch over the door of your lips, and pray for those symptoms to leave and come under the subjection of Christ.

Unforgiveness

Protect your heart; never give Satan access to your body. Do not hold on to unforgiveness, it is cancerous and will destroy you. Unforgiveness blocks the flow of the anointing. Yes, we are human. Yes, we hurt. Sometimes, it is hard to look past what has happened to us by the hands of others. Let us remember what was done to Jesus. He endured several lashes, public ridicule, and death – just for us. Nothing anyone will ever do to us can compare to what was done to Christ. I know we do not always think about that when we are going through something. Let us follow Jesus' example, and stay free. Let us be reminded, although they certainly may not always feel like light afflictions at the time, that Jesus said that they were *"but for a moment, [and] works for us a far more exceeding and eternal weight of glory,"* (***2 Corinthians 4:17***).

I believe Paul had some terrible things happen to him, but he called them light. When Stephen was being stoned to death, he asked the Father not to lay this to their charge. I believe some of us would be throwing rocks and running for our lives, if we had things of that nature to happen to us. Stephen looked up and saw Jesus standing at the right hand of the Father. I believe Jesus gave Stephen a standing ovation, because He was proud of the stand he took. How many of us can say that Jesus is proud of the stands we are taking when it comes to forgiveness?

Unforgiveness opens doors for stress. Stress causes our cell receptors to become weak, thus, allowing free radicals to flow throughout our bodies causing attacks of sickness, pain, and disease. I am sure you have heard this statement so many times before, "Unforgiveness is like drinking poison and waiting for the other person to die." But, it is true; it is detrimental for us. When we walk around with a forgiving heart, a forgiving nature, we get freedom and access to the Father without hindrances. We do not want our prayers to be hindered in any capacity, whether on our jobs, in our homes, in our schools, or in our churches, because we refuse to walk in forgiveness toward each other. How many of us can say, without a shadow of doubt, that some of our aches in our hearts, minds, souls, and bodies are not caused by the unwillingness to forgive?

Finances

In reading the context in Luke 16:10, we concur that it is talking about finances. It states, "He that is faithful in that which is least is faithful also in much: and he that is unjust in the least is unjust also in much." Jesus said the least thing to believe God for is finances. If we cannot believe for the least, the smallest, how can we believe for the greater, such as healing, casting out devils, etc.? Satan does not want us to promote the Word of God through our giving, tithes, and offerings. Money is simply a medium of exchange; it is not your life. Faith is your medium of exchange in the spirit realm. God said to the givers in **Philippians 4:19** that *he would supply all their needs according to His riches in glory by Christ Jesus*. That is according to His riches, and not your paycheck. Satan does not want you to participate in giving. If you consider Satan's attacks, you will not give. Yet, this is another one of his plots to slow or stop the work of God from going forth.

The Family Unit

God has set order in the family unit, and everyone has a position to uphold. However, the world's system has crept into the church and the Body of Christ has accepted these worldly standards. In **Ephesians 5:23-25**, God was clear about the roles of spouses and *how those husbands and wives should treat each other*. Today, people falling away from God, society has deemed it acceptable for kids to have two mommies or two daddies that have wed in matrimony. This is a work of the enemy to distort God's position on families. In fact, Satan knows that strong, godly families make strong churches. It is no secret that the spirit of separation and divorce are running rampant throughout the church. It seems to be at an even rate of speed, statistically, as it is in the secular world. The world's way is every man for himself. Do what feels good to you in that moment. Therefore, if the church adopts that mentality, undoubtedly, that will lead to self-centeredness and division, thus creating disharmony and divorces, because we give the enemy access. **Philippians 2:3** says, "*Let nothing be done through strife or vainglory, but in lowliness of mind let each esteem others better than themselves.*"

Selfish Gratification

Selfish gratification can occur in various forms. Perhaps, it is the greed of money, power, or even lust. This can cause a lot of hurt in church also. Imagine having pastors looking from the pulpit, not really examining the souls of the individuals, but mainly seeing them as potential prospects for their earthly desires – whether financial, sexual, or control. This can definitely injure God's precious flock. There is a price to be paid when we are in leadership. Our job as pastors is to protect the sheep and seek God's wisdom daily on matters concerning them. Jesus paid the price for all of us. He shed His blood for us all. To trample on the sheep is a serious indictment. Self-gratification is not just limited to some pastors being used by Satan, but any member or nonmember of the church, who use their position of authority to distort the love of Christ.

At this very moment, as I write these words to you, I feel a strong urge to tell you more about the relationship between the Pastor that I have been speaking about and me. This was indeed a learning experience, and I cannot keep what I am about to tell you a secret any longer. I am willing to divulge a shameful part of my journey with you, in hopes that it will help others who may have experienced or is experiencing what I am about to share. But, I will go back a little further so that you can connect the dots. For years, my family of five, which included my husband, my three children, and I were seeking a ministry that would teach us to truly understand and expound upon the Word of God. When we came upon that ministry, we immediately joined. At that moment, we felt that our prayers were answered. For the first two years, we all were active in that church, and did whatever the Pastor needed us to do.

I believed that the father-daughter relationship that I had with the Pastor was very strong. I attributed that to my diligence in serving. I was and still am a person that tries my very best. I wanted to make my spiritual father (the Pastor) and his ministry look good. Because of that, I believed that was why he would often smile and refer to me as his gem.

In our third year in this ministry, we noticed a change. Undoubtedly, this change altered my life for many years. Mom always taught me to honor and respect men and women of God. She would advise me to serve them because they are God's representatives. This advice, in my opinion, became a weakness for me. There were no spoken or unspoken boundaries. Therefore, Satan was able to use this against me. Because I was a shy introvert who did not like confrontation, it was easy for me to smile and say yes in agreement just to satisfy others.

As the director of the Intercessory Prayer Ministry, whenever we held a revival in a city, I would go one or two days before the services started so that I could pray for the services. I remember the Pastor's son made a comment to me saying, "Why is it that everywhere my dad is, you are there?" My reply to him was to pray and support the ministry. Whenever there was a meeting in my city, the Pastor would stay at our home. I did not think it was inappropriate to have my Pastor in our home when my husband was not there; after all, he is the Pastor. I was so blind! I fell prey to sexual manipulation and coercion at 32 years old. That was when my first sexual contact happened with the Pastor. It was on my 10th wedding anniversary, while my husband was working a 24-hour shift as a firefighter.

At that time, I was young in age and relatively new to the things of God. "Some things you need to take to the grave" is what the Pastor would often say to me. I think back to how impressionable I was. I followed him no matter what he said or did. If you are thinking, "That's just stupid. You have a brain. You should have used it." Believe me; I do not blame you for thinking that. Sometimes, it is very easy to say what we would do, until we are actually in that position.

As a pastor myself, I look back on that period of my life and see how as a sheep I was not being protected. I find it rather disturbing how easily manipulated I was. I pray healing for others who have experienced this level, or any level of manipulation and control at the hands of their pastors. There is absolutely no way that you can pastor and minister God's Word effectively and sleep with the sheep. I was so naïve and oblivious to what was happening around me. As I look back now, before the sexual activities occurred, I realize that there were warnings all the time. But, I was not thinking that anything on that level could or would ever occur. There were female members who left the ministry. They would call me and say things, without saying things, if you know what I mean. They would warn me to be careful with my interactions with the Pastor. Yet, I still did not see it coming. No way things like this would ever happen in the church; well, that's what I thought. After all, I thought there was nothing to be concerned about. He was my spiritual father. Wow, I was wrong indeed.

When my eyes finally opened, I no longer saw him as my spiritual father, but as my enemy. He knew I was vulnerable and in a bad marriage situation. I believe he used my wounds as a green light to gain power, thus abusing his authority. ABUSE OF POWER, CONTROL,

INTIMIDATION, but worse of all, TRANSFER OF SPIRIT! Those words ran rampantly through my mind, pierced my heart, and trampled my soul. My character began to change. Guilt and condemnation lived within me. He used manipulation and mind control to get me to think that this was solely my fault. He would ask, "Why did you do this to me?" I will not deny that my flesh enjoyed the pleasure from our experiences. But, this was merely the trap of Satan. After some time, it got to the point where I hated being with him. I would literally vomit afterwards. I remember asking the Pastor very matter-of-factly, "How do I stop this from happening?" "How do I get out of this situation?" His reply was, "You can't!" When I heard those two words, somehow, it gave me the strength to move forward. "No one tells me I can't do a thing," is what I boldly proclaimed to myself.

My husband knew a change had taken place. He knew something was not right. I later confessed to him what was going on. He never confronted the Pastor, but he did lose all interest in the ministry, but he kept going because of my involvement in the church. He never developed a rapport with the Pastor. In July 2009, my husband went home to be with Jesus. One month after the death of my husband, I spoke with the Pastor about the grief I was experiencing. His reply was simply callous. "What is it? You can't get over him?" is what he said in a condescending, rather cold-hearted tone.

Lust and selfish gratification can be very destructive. Seeds of doubt were planted in my mind between what was right and wrong. My marriage, ministry, and life changed the moment my thinking changed. I began to think that it was okay to live an immoral life. Besides, the Pastor does it, is what I reasoned with myself as a justification. God is using the Pastor mightily, even in immorality, is what I thought. Absolutely, my marriage was having its challenges. I felt that the Pastor saw the vulnerability and played on it. Definitely, engaging in this relationship with the Pastor was a bad choice. It worsened my situation and it cost me tremendously. But, God is a restorer. Before my husband's death, we were able to reconcile. The last years of our marriage, I believe, were our best.

Indeed, Satan's plots are real, and he will go to whatever lengths to destroy the Body of Christ. We have to remember that Jesus is the Savior. His body was attacked for the cross, and then He was put on the cross. However, his crucifixion and resurrection are what allows us to make it day by day through Satan's attacks in and out of or homes. We need testimonies that God can heal our homes. When we allow bitterness to take root, we are giving the prince of this world access to strike. We need to do as the scripture says and have nothing in us that Satan can use as an arsenal against us. I think we should ask ourselves daily, "Is there anything in my life or in my character that Satan can use to attach himself to and/or get control of me?" We should search ourselves daily, and ask God to search us, as well. We need to make every effort to find out if we have given the enemy access in words, action, or deeds.

•   •   •   •   •   •   •   •   •   •

DON'T BLAME GOD
Chapter 5

According to **Ephesians 2:2**, *Satan is called the prince of the power of the air, who works in the children of disobedience.* Although Satan's power is limited in comparison to the almighty God, make no mistake, his demons have been given the power to rule kingdoms of darkness. When bad things happen, we cannot be so quick to say God did it. Yes, God allows things to happen. But, we should not give God credit and blame Him for Satan's destructive acts. Satan throws his rocks and hides his hands.

Satan has his hands in controlling catastrophes. Every time there are hurricanes, floods, or other storms, many have said, "Oh, look what God did to us." There is even a clause in insurance policies that states when tragedies and natural disasters strike, they are considered "Acts of God." God and His Word are one. God will never go contrary to His Word. In **Genesis 9:15**, it tells us *"the waters shall no more become a flood to destroy all flesh."*

We must build a relationship with Christ and

read our Bible. God is not responsible for every bad thing that happens in your life. Yes, He allowed it. But, He is not the author of confusion. Religion tells us to never ask God why or even question Him. It is true that God never makes mistakes. In **James 4:2**, …*We have not because we ask not*. If we need answers, we can ask the Father. He is our Father. He wants to communicate with us on a regular basis. He says *if any man lacks wisdom, let him ask me, and I will give it to him* **(James 1:5)**. When Christians do not know these truths, they begin to ask God questions like, "Why don't you do something about my hurt? Why did you let this happen?"

God's authority and His power are carried out through His body – the church. If we refuse to exercise the authority He has given us, there will be no change. When we fail to understand these principles, many of us begin to blame God. Victory is in our hands and our mouths. We need to *speak those things that are not as though they were* **(Romans 4:17)**. When God gives us instructions and we fail to carry them out, we can only blame ourselves.

To live in this Earth, you will need a physical earthly body. Jesus gave up His earthly body, when He became the blood sacrifice for our sins.

We are also part spirit. Just imagine how awesome that is to have the Spirit of Christ operating within us, when we accept Him as our Lord and Savior. He gives us authority, as a result. Think back to the abundance and authority that were first given to Adam. Because of disobedience, he lost those things. A part of his authority was to rule and reign in the Earth. Jesus, often called the second Adam, regained the authority, and gave it to the body, which is us, and said, "Now, you rule and reign." He still expects us to rule and reign. Therefore, if we refuse to exercise the Word, we fall beneath our rights and privileges. ***Colossians 1:18*** says, *He is the head...* But, His headship and authority are exercised through His body, you the believer.

Do not limit yourself in thinking that the pastor is the only one who hears from God. ***Hosea 4:6*** clearly states that, *"My people are destroyed for lack of knowledge."* We put so much emphasis on our leader, oftentimes, failing to seek God ourselves. I am not saying that we should not hold our leaders in high esteem. Let us not forget that I, too, am a pastor. But, we should never put anyone before God. Making others an idol and wanting to become just like them will be a mistake. God uniquely and creatively designed each one of us. We should only strive to exemplify Christ in all that we are and in all that we do.

On countless occasions of heartbreak and disappointments, do we realize that our leaders have a flesh also that they have to bring under the subjection of Christ? When we see those that we put all our hope and trust into are caught in a moral failure, we get disappointed. We can become so broken to the point where we do not trust any pastors or any churches. This is not what God wants for us. Satan uses those incidents to break our spirit. We cannot blame God because a fallible creature did not meet our expectations or walk in a manner that we feel is pleasing to God or us. We need to redirect our focus. Seek God for yourselves. Do not simply rely on what the pastor is saying from the pulpit. Read and study those scriptures for yourself. Pray for wisdom, understanding, and guidance. Ask God for interpretation, when you are confused. It is of utmost importance that we renew our mind by the Word of God. It is a matter of life and spiritual death, sometimes even physical death.

Some people have confessed that they believe that God put hurt or sickness on them to teach them a lesson. They go on to say, "The hand of

God is on me." Quite honestly, we have done things to our own bodies and have not taken care of them properly that have warranted some sicknesses. We cannot make God the culprit for every bad thing that has occurred in our lives. Let every man, woman, boy, and girl examine themselves to see where they let sin creep in. Let us also change our thinking. Instead of saying that God's hands are on us to punish us, let us say by His stripes we are healed. Let us say we pray His hands are on us to wipe all manner of disease out of our body. Words have power!

We can overcome hurt. ***James 1:21*** tells us to *"get rid of all moral filth and the evil that is so prevalent and humbly accept the word planted in you, which can save you."* Do you know what that means? That means the Word will save our souls! Victory is on the inside of us! We have to activate it by the Word of God and by our faith! Glory be to God! Our minds were not automatically renewed when we received salvation. We, however, became new creatures. Salvation and mind renewal are continual processes that must be worked on daily.

God is looking for someone whose heart is blameless toward Him. He wants to show Himself strong on our behalf. You might be saying, where is God? Doesn't He care? The problem is not God. The problem often lies within us. He is waiting on us. He said He is an ever-present God in the time of trouble. We have to call on Him, and He will answer. If you are not calling on Him perhaps, we are having a problem with communication. Are we in a one-side relationship when it comes to God? Could it be that we are often not calling God, but blaming Him instead? When we know the true nature of God, we will not blame Him. If He gave His only son for us, while we were yet still sinners, why would we possibly think for even a second that He does not love us and just wants to inflict pain upon us? It is not His character. He is a loving Father. Do not get me wrong. He is a true Father. Consequences for our actions or misdeeds will occur, if our actions are contrary to His Word. It is important to acknowledge His love and care for us. God is always speaking. But, are we always listening?

• • • • • • • • • •

PASTOR'S ABANDONMENT
Chapter 6

When you think of abandonment, the first thing comes to mind is someone who leaves without notice, and sometimes never return. How many of you have ever felt abandoned, lonely, and destitute? As a child of God, I can tell you that we never have to deal with abandonment from God, our Father. When He says *He will never leave us or forsake us*, He means it (**Hebrews 13:5b**). God is not like man, *He will not and cannot lie* (**Numbers 23:19**). I can truly say that I felt abandoned by my Pastor. I sensed the leading of the Lord to start a ministry, and although I have been a faithful, dedicated, devoted, and loyal servant for many years, I was met with opposition. I am not saying that everyone should just start planting churches around the world, because they want to make a name for themselves or they are pretending that they heard from the Lord. When you have sought the face of God for your next level in ministry and He has released you, you must do what He tells you to do.

That was not always an easy thing for me to

do. It was hard dealing with those seasoned members. Particularly those who knew the voice of God, operated in the gifts, and knew how to sense God's leading. Seasoned Christians generally pray and seek the face of God, then take whatever information or direction they were given in prayer to their pastors for a blessing. So, what happens when the pastor isn't in agreement with what you believe God is saying? How do you feel when they tell you to wait a year, two years, or even longer just to see if it really is God? What do you do when you come back within those time frames or longer and they are still not convinced that you really heard from the Lord?

In that instance, I found myself with no blessing from the Pastor, no preparation for my exit, and now the topic of his sermon entitled, "Rebellion." I felt he was referring to me, because he revealed personal information about me in the sermon, but without saying my name. I had all kind of scriptures thrown at me by him. But, I decided to follow my heart in what I believed God was directing me to do. I looked at all the years I spent as a dedicated member, and how much time I spent learning the leading of the Holy Spirit and being rooted and grounded in the Word. I believed that it was time for me to put into practice what I had learned over the years. I approached him with questions about the call on my life. He replied that God was waiting for me to get my business together. I never really knew what that meant. He never pointed out what I needed to get together. As a result, that statement caused even more confusion. I felt sad when the one who should have been at my side giving me instructions and helping me with the directions of my life was not there...my Pastor. I walked away from a work feeling unsupported, abandoned, and alone.

Perhaps, you may be wondering about the Pastor's abandonment part and thinking to yourself, "Well, the Pastor did not leave; she left the Pastor and the church." When attempting to start any kind of kingdom work, you need your leader for guidance. If they are not there, you are left on your own feeling abandoned. What do you do in a situation like this? You love God, and you love your leader. In many instances, your leader has become like a father or mother to you. This is demonstrated loyalty. But, what about the destiny God has designed for you? After waiting for a blessing that may or may not ever come from the leader, there is a possibility that you may begin to resent the time you wasted waiting for man's blessing and approval.

The Word says, "*We ought to obey God rather than man*" *(Acts 5:29)*. I am a true believer that where God leads, He feeds; and where He guides, He provides. Test the spirit by the spirit. If it is of God, it will stand; and if it is of man, it will come to naught – nothing. In situations like these, if you do not have a relationship with God, you will be crushed. Let me speak of an individual I served in ministry with. Let us call him Tom. We were a part of the same ministry for years. Tom served for nearly twenty years, whereas, I served thirty-one years. Tom was anointed of God. But, I believe his downfall came when he seemed to worship the ground the Pastor walked on. Tom and the Pastor had a difference of opinion, thus, resulting in Tom leaving the church. Tom took it pretty hard and began enjoying the party lifestyle and vowing never to set foot or enter in another church door. Whatever the hurt he experienced, it went deep enough to damage Tom to the core. If we do not keep focus on Christ, we will lose our way. **Psalm 118:8** says, "*It is better to trust in the Lord than to put confidence in man.*" When we are out of balance, destructive things can happen.

I am a pastor. I have had people to tell me that they love me, only to walk away and spread false information about the ministry or me. I also realize that I cannot do anything about their actions. I have to move on, because I am only responsible for my own actions. My responsibility as a pastor, the under-shepherd, is to feed God's sheep. When they walk away deciding that they choose not to get any more feeding under my leadership, I must demonstrate maturity. I cannot add salt to the wound and begin preaching against their actions. They may already be hurt or confused and hoping this is the place that's going to lead them to their destiny. I do believe it is wrong and ungodly to tell God's people not to associate with those who left the church, particularly with those who are just following the leading of the spirit for ministry purpose. But, if one was ex-communicated, I believe that is a different issue. I learned from what happened to me, and I tried not to repeat it in my ministry. Before anyone answers the call to pastoring, please make sure you know it IS God, without an inkling of doubt. Please, seek the consult of a reputable man or woman of God. I believe God has counted me faithful and His promises for my life are yay and amen. I am now entering my fifth year of pastoring. To God Be the Glory!

·………·

REVEALING A PASTOR'S HEART
Chapter 7

I do believe it is wrong to judge a person, by saying that you know why they did what they did. You can judge the actions, but you cannot judge what is in the heart. Only the Holy Spirit knows the heart of man. Moreover, only He can reveal the matters of the heart. We can examine the outside, and even the fruit that we see. I do believe the eye will reveal the soul, which consists of one's mind, will, emotions, imaginations, and intellect. Sometimes, we tend to judge people on how we would respond to certain situations. We may respond to things a certain way. Is it fair to expect others to respond the same way as us? We have to remember that we all have different mindsets and may be at a different level of maturity and faith in Christ. The Bible tells us that if we have a difference of opinion, or a disagreement, to go to that person and try to rectify the problem. If that does not work, then we are to get witnesses and go to the church.

Just like everyone, we, as pastors will have to deal with issues from time to time. We may be vulnerable and susceptible to physical and emotional attacks just like everyone else. Although those issues may be present, we are still called to help the people. We are still called to protect the sheep, and feed them with knowledge and understanding. I have a visual illustration of the pastor being the ring finger who are married to the people. Sometimes, we see the good, the bad, and the ugly. However, we still need to be godly examples. Communication, camaraderie, and fellowship must exist within a pastor-member relationship. We must talk the talk and walk the walk. Here is another illustration of my view of church. The shepherd has a staff. One hand is a hoop to draw the sheep in when they go astray. The other end is pointed. He uses this end to jab the sheep, to get their attention. I have noticed that pastors, who operate in transparency, tend to have members who feel more confident in following them as they follow Christ. I believe it is important to show the people that we are approachable. People do not care how much you know, until they know how much you care.

Leadership, in the church, is responsible and accountable to God and the pastor. Because God is a God of order, order in churches should exist. There is protocol for addressing matters or asking questions. Well-meaning people, because of the propensity in us to be the humans that we are, can start out doing what's right, but end up gossiping, murmuring, complaining, and spreading assumptions which can cause discord among the people.

Let us be clear, hurts do not always come from the pastor. Sometimes, it's from other members or others in authority positions, such as deacons, ministers, or even ushers and greeters. Sometimes, there are members who do not understand the office and think they can do a better job. Misunderstandings can occur at any rate and at any level. We live in a world where sin exists. There is a propensity for hurt and offense to occur no matter where you go.

God ordains all authority. The pastor is God's delegated authority. A pastor's job is to tell you what God is saying about the situation. It is up to the congregants for how they receive it. The pastor's job is not to make the decision for you, but to give you the counsel of God. So, what happens when what the pastor is saying is not in line with what your plan is? Do you just disagree, get mad, and leave? Do you say, "I'm a man or woman, just like you? I am grown. I make my own decisions." Absolutely, the ultimate decision is yours. God will never override a person's will. Do you think it is wiser to talk to the Father and pursue godly counsel in matters? It is important for Christians of all levels to examine themselves to determine if it is God, or their flesh, not just for ministry sake, but also for everything.

As pastors, we should never take offences personally. We must remember it is not about us, but it is about people walking in darkness. Our job is to show them the light of Christ. If you are hurt or mad at your pastor, examine the situation, seek God's direction, and follow His leading for healing and deliverance. Allow God to give you clear instructions on what to do with that matter. Perhaps, He may tell you to let it go, or even confront the issue. It is important to know without any doubt that you are following God's instructions on a matter. Remember, **1 Chronicles 6:22** says, "*Touch not mine anointed, and do my prophets no harm.*" It would not be a good idea to lay false charges against God's elect.

God is a God of purpose. If you prayed that your pastor's heart be revealed in a matter, and you were shown that they're being destructive which will not be for your good, your next step is to pray for the courage to do God's will. God will always guide you in doing what is right. If you are a victim of any type of pastoral abuse, including physical abuse, sexual abuse, or emotional abuse, you need to do more than just pray. My advice to you is to run for your life. Do not allow your loyalty to the leader who is doing this to you, to trump your loyalty to Christ and the respect you should have for yourself. God does not orchestrate this form of manipulation. That pastor is not respecting the oath of the clergy, or God's people. Please, be wise and not let the scripture referring to love covers a multitude of sins be taken out of context for their own personal gratifications.

There may be times when we misjudge the heart of the pastor by calling it bondage. Or, maybe God has revealed the sincerity of your pastor's heart. If that is the case, do not allow anyone to poison you against that revelation. Once you receive the revelation, this is not the time to engage in gossiping (or any time for that matter). Gossiping is casual or unconstrained conversations or reports about other people, typically involving details that are not confirmed. Gossips generally disagree with something or someone. Gossips have an eloquent way of putting their spin on things. Unfortunately, in my case, God's revelation of my Pastor's heart was not so positive. I had to get the courage to go through the proper channels to leave.

I praise God that He did bring me through the yelling and the hurt that I incurred. Correction, love, and forgiveness are the three words that I live by that have helped me to navigate through life.

• • • • • • • • • •

MASTERING YOUR EMOTIONS
Chapter 8

We need to know the role emotions play in our lives. It is equally important to know how to take control of them. Yes, we have experienced hurt. Now, what are we going to do about it? God promised to keep us in perfect peace if our minds are stayed on Him. If we focus too much on the hurt, we can miss God. We will never be able to overcome the pain, if we continue to keep rehearsing repeatedly about what happened to us. Torments in our minds, bodies, and souls are because of our refusal to let something go.

When we allow our thinking to control our emotions that means we are not mastering our emotions. To get a grip on the potential stress that may come, we must change our thoughts. Doing so, in a positive way, will change our lives. Let us minimize our stress level, by eliminating stressors, such as these dangerously fueled emotions. It is time to let the hurt or abuse go! When we are emotionally ruled, we become dangerous to ourselves and to others. We are not being ruled by what the Word is saying when we allow that to happen. Rather, we are ruled by our emotions, which is the opposite of faith.

Emotions do not know reality. They act out what we give them permission to do. When we replay the hurt over and over, our mind gets fixated on it, and therein, is where we give our strength and power. Meditating on that negative emotion day and night can be self-destructive. God instructs us to meditate on His word day and night. If we hold a thought for 17 seconds or more, another thought just like it will join it. Imagine when those two thoughts come together, how explosive it could be, thus making it more powerful. That means two negative thoughts put together will create a mind that can erode with burdens. Just imagine what two positive thoughts could do. When our minds get full, we have now brought forth the birth of a new thought. ***2 Corinthians 10:5*** eloquently says *to cast those negative thoughts down*. Otherwise, they will become strongholds, and we will now have a fight on our hands. Our fight is really in our minds, which is where the battlefield really is. Satan wants us to abandon the promises of God, so he uses our minds by constantly reminding us of the hurts we endured in and out of church.

I do not want to be insensitive to any hurts

that you have experienced. Hurt is hurt, regardless of the nature and longevity of the hurt. It may be possible that being more alive to the flesh than to the Spirit of God allows us to get hurt more easily and to carry offenses longer. Pride and self-centeredness can often enter the picture when we continue to talk about how we're hurt and how we feel. We develop the "all about me" syndrome. **Proverbs 13:10** says, *"Only by pride comes contention."*

God gave us emotions, and they have a role in our lives. But, we should never allow them to rule us. If we want to change and we no longer want to be controlled by our emotions, we must put God's Word into action. We must meditate on it, speak it, and refuse to allow negative thoughts to imprison us. If we practice this, it will produce what we desire. It is now time for us to make our emotions submit to us, rather than the other way around. Making decisions during turmoil is not always a good idea. We may discover that we have made choices out of our flesh because of our emotions, and inherently, made wrong decisions. We need to be sensitively aware that the human mind cannot function at its maximum best, when there are overcharged emotions. Only when the mind is still, will it work in a smooth and well-organized function. Let us not make another decision solely based on our emotions. Let me be absolutely clear, we cannot serve God in our emotions. Emotions change from time to time. While it is true, the love we may show or have for God will make us emotional, as we may cry in joy, dance, or scream with excitement, but serving God or people purely out of emotionalism, it could turn volatile.

When we mentally take charge of our minds, we can decide that we will no longer be moved by what we see or feel, but by the Word of our almighty God. Remember, we must be stronger than our emotions.

FREEDOM THROUGH FORGIVENESS
Chapter 9

Matthew 5:44 says, *"But I say unto you, love your enemies, bless them that curse you, do good to them that hate you, and pray for them which despitefully use you, and persecute you."* To be honest, my flesh wanted nothing to do with that verse, when I went through that hurt in church. I wanted to react to the flesh, and not the spirit. It was hard for me to forgive this hurt immediately, mainly because so much was happening at once. I guess I expected a, "Hey, go for it. Build the kingdom" response from the Pastor as I was leaving to enter Bible College. I think the shocking part was that he never personally told me how he felt. Of course, I was in disbelief that I did not even get a goodbye. I can never remember having to deal with something this painful and hurtful. It felt like a parent abandoning a child and cutting the apron strings and saying, "Hey, you're on your own." I was angry because I felt I gave 31 years of my life, and it meant nothing to him. I walked out of the church that Sunday, asking myself, "What just happened?"

It is important that whatever we do in life or ministry, we must do it heartily as to the Lord, and not unto men. The Lord revealed to me that not everything I did was lost and that the bank accounts rolled over into the ministry He has given me. Praise Jesus! Satan used this hurt to hold me in bondage, but because I served God those 31 years and not man, that bondage was broken from my life.

This all happened the first Sunday in August 2010; one year, and one month after my husband of 33 years transitioned to heaven. The next day, I was scheduled for an outpatient procedure, a hernia repair. Keep in mind that I was still confused, angry, and could not even think clearly. I could not hear God because of all the madness that clogged my mind up. In **John 14:30**, Jesus told his disciples, *the prince of this world cometh, and had nothing in me*. He was saying there is nothing in me Satan can use to destroy me. But, I knew I had stuff in me…anger, hurt, and resentment. I resented the Pastor's cruel treatment toward me. As a child of God, I knew this was not the attitude to have, but I was very angry. The Word says in **Ephesians 4:26**, "*Be angry, but sin not.*" My anger became sin, when it turned into unforgiveness. This gave Satan residence in my life.

After my surgery, for seven months, I was in and out of the hospital. A simple procedure turned into months of agony, nausea, and any smell made me sick. If I did not eat small portions, I would throw the food back up. The incision kept opening and releasing a foul smell. Doctors had to cut me open to drain the inflammation. Finally, on the seventh month, after surgery, I had another operation to remove the hernia mesh that my body kept rejecting.

I was holding on to unforgiveness, and being destroyed, as a result. I knew I had to forgive the Pastor for his actions toward me. I am not saying it was easy. It was probably one of the hardest things I ever had to do. All I could see was 31 years of service. I had a choice to become bitter or better. My flesh did not want to let go of the hurt. In chapter eight, I spoke about rehearsing the pain and meditating on the hurt, which only makes the stronghold harder to deal with. I knew I had to forgive at some point in my life, so I did. It was not easy. I had to keep telling myself I forgive him. Of course, my feelings did not want to line up with my words. I realized I had to keep confessing and getting control of my emotions. There were times it felt like my flesh was winning, but I was determined not to accept what seemed like an apparent defeat in the flesh. The real secret to winning is never to quit! I finally got to a place where the hurt no longer had a sting in my life. I attribute that to an act of willing myself to forgive him.

Unforgiveness was Satan's plot to destroy me. The doctors told me after the last surgery in March 2011 that I needed up to six months to heal. I was instructed to return after that length of time, in order to have my stomach reconstructed. I already had plans to enroll in Bible College in another state. That really was a tough thing to handle. What do you do in a situation like this? Seeing how hard Satan fought to stop me, I now knew I had no choice but to follow God's plan for my life. During my healing process, I could hardly sit for thirty minutes. Six months later, in September 2011, I packed enough belongings that I would need for college into my Lincoln Town Car. Prior to leaving Columbia, South Carolina, I contacted a couple in Colorado who both were graduates of Charis Bible College. They rented a huge home to use as a dormitory for students relocating to have a place to stay. They secured my room for arrival within three days.

This was a difficult drive considering I could

only sit for a short period of time. I knew the drive would be a challenge. But, it was a challenge that I was up for. I knew God was leading and guiding me, and that gave me the strength and comfort that I needed to make the trip. I had no doubt in my mind. I knew I could do it with His help. On the first day, I drove seven hours. I drove for eight hours on the second day. On the third day, I drove for nine hours. God supernaturally sustained me. I spent most of my trip fellowshipping with Jesus.

It was definitely my faith in God that allowed me to drive across the country to Colorado Springs. I knew that the college had two enrollment dates, one in September and the other one in November. I did not have the fees I needed to complete the enrollment process into Charis Bible College for the September date, but I went anyway. Orientation, at Charis Bible College, was called Rally Day. This day was designated for enrollment, paying fees, getting books, meeting & greeting other students and the instructors. I planned to wait until I got all my fees, before signing up for the November date. I worked as a caregiver at a senior care facility in Columbia. Because the company was nationwide, I was able to get a transfer to Colorado Springs.

Although the transfer was in progress when I left Columbia, it did take a few weeks before they could place me in the facility. I did not know how many hours I needed to work to obtain the exact amount of fees I needed so that I could officially enroll and start my classes under the leadership of Andrew Wommack. Amid wondering how long it would take, I received a phone call from the couple I was living with. They instructed me not to miss the rally. At the time, they were out of town. I did as they asked me to and attended Rally Day. I will never forget that day. It was on a Monday when Andrew Wommack spoke to us and I was able to meet some of the instructors. Although I was now fired up and excited, I knew that I could not start until November because of financial reasons. I spoke to the Lord, and I reminded Him that He told me to come to Colorado at that exact time. I also reminded Him that I did that by faith and that I obeyed. On my way home, I made a stop to open a bank account. Upon returning to my car, I received another phone call. This time it was from the administrator informing me that an anonymous person paid all my fees totaling $1,200. Tears began to flow nonstop. Eventually, I found out that the couple that I was staying with paid my fees. They wanted to make sure my needs were met. They truly were like family to me. I am so grateful to God for using them to help me. I am also thankful for their obedience.

My first year at college was successful. The couple I stayed with eventually gave up the boarding house. I made plans to leave Colorado Springs and transfer to Charis Bible College in Charlotte, North Carolina for my second year of school. Besides, I really missed my family and I wanted to be close to home. In my spirit, I did not feel I was getting a release to leave Colorado. I know it was the leading of the Holy Spirit, because the school's director in Charlotte resigned before the school opened that year. Now, I had no choice but to remain in Colorado where the rent was expensive. Ironically, that college in Charlotte opened back up one year later. It continues to thrive to this very day.

During college, there was a young woman in my class, who always came around me. She always wanted us to go shopping or eating together. I was focused only on surviving, and not on fellowshipping. After some time, I finally gave in to her request for hanging out together. Lo, and behold, I did not realize that our interactions were God's supernatural intervention. She told me that she heard I was not going to do my second year of school in Colorado. I told her that was true, but that God said he was not finished with me in Colorado. I also told her that I was interested in renting an apartment. At that very moment, she got excited. She told me that her tri-level home had a third floor with a fully furnished two-bedroom apartment that they rent to college students. To make a long story short, I moved in. I made one rent payment and began to realize that tuition was more than I could handle. She and her husband decided to have a meeting with me to tell what they believed God told them. They told me not to worry about payment for rent or utilities, and just focus on my job and tuition. For a year, I lived without the stress and worry of rent and utilities. They were the second family who blessed me in Colorado. The amazing thing about this experience is that the couple never got a renter for the second bedroom. Therefore, I had the apartment all to myself. I am just thinking about all the provisions that the Lord made for me in Colorado. Although it was many years ago, I still honor Him for everything He did there.

I truly believe that when we walk in forgiveness, God will open doors so that blessings will shower upon us. I am a true believer that where God guides, He provides. As I sat under the teaching of Andrew Wommack, God reconstructed my stomach. God completely healed me. God's Word was medicine. I am now seven years healed by the stripes of Jesus Christ. Unforgiveness gave Satan access to my life. Forgiveness toward the Pastor stripped the bondage off me. I regained my freedom, and God healed me through forgiveness.

MY RESURRECTION
Chapter 10

I believe sometimes we want the testimony, but without the test. Unfortunately, they often go hand in hand. One cannot exist without the other. Jesus, in ***John 4:4***, went through Samaria. As a result, He met a woman at a well. He ministered everlasting life and salvation to her. In return, she went into the city spreading the good news of the gospel. This turned into a two-day revival. We must die and empty ourselves of anything that might stand in the way of the Holy Spirit being able to work in and through us. Paul reminded us that we must die daily to self. I am talking about putting our flesh under subjection to the Word of Christ daily.

Until we become that corn of wheat that falls into the ground and die, we will not bring forth fruit. The Father is glorified when we bear fruit. It is impossible to bear fruit when all you feel is hurt. Even though I loved God, the situation with the Pastor made me see that my flesh did not want to cooperate. It was screaming bloody murder! The sustaining force that kept me above water was my relationship with the Father. I knew He loved me, because my Mom taught me this as a little girl. Although I knew this, I still felt nothing but hurt. I thank God that His love for us is not based on a feeling, but on His Word.

I had conflicting feelings, but I refused to die and let the hurt overcome me. I would not glorify the Father, nor bring forth fruit, if I gave in like that. In my mind, I decided the fight would be on. But, I needed to renew my mind and walk in what the Holy Spirit revealed to me. When I changed my thoughts, my life changed. Why? Well, it simply was because I stopped meditating on the hurt. Then, and only then, did God begin to open new roads to my destiny.

To me, I was good. But, then the first thing God said was that my flesh was not dead enough, because dead men do not feel a thing. I decided to toughen up and rise above the reproach I was dealing with. Once I received revelation that glorifying the Father brings forth fruit, I knew I really needed to die daily and stop loving my life more than anything else. After making that decision, I began to experience an intimacy with God like never before. I always knew He loved me, but this was on another level. Sometimes, we think we are waiting on God, but God is waiting on us.

In ***James 4:8***, I understood that *if I draw near to God, He would draw near to me*. When I began to do just that, the hurt began to disappear. I began to pray for the Pastor and his ministry. I have learned that if you will die daily, fall into the ground like wheat, figuratively, of course, Jesus will raise you up. This is the first step to being resurrected from your apparent defeat. If God be with you, who can be against you? ***Matthew 10:39*** says, "*Whoever finds his life will lose it, and whoever loses his life for my sake will find it.*"

Perhaps, you may be going through a current situation that may feel like hell. But, if you surrender and remember what Jesus said in ***Acts 2:27***, you will realize that *He will not leave your soul to rot in that place*. Resurrection Sunday is coming, if you do not quit! I am a living testimony, because God resurrected me from my personal hell. In order to be resurrected, I knew that I first had to lose my life. I had to reject the things, thoughts, and actions that God would not be pleased with. Today, God is using me in ministry. I am glorifying Him and bringing forth fruit for His kingdom. A price must be paid, before you can receive the goods. But, Jesus already paid it on the cross. The only thing you should do, if you have not already, is to accept Jesus Christ as your Lord and Savior, trust Him, surrender to Him, obey Him, and follow Him.

• • • • • • • • • •

YOU ARE AN OVERCOMER
Chapter 11

Genesis 1:26 says, *we are made in the image and likeness of God.* In this world, we are not always going to experience great situations, if you have not found out already. In fact, some are going to be quite terrible situations. But, we must be of good cheer, because according to ***John 16:33,*** *Jesus overcame the world*, making us a world overcomer because we were born of Him. Jesus told us that if they persecuted Him, they would also persecute us. Yes, we are overcomers, because greater is He that is in us, than he that is in the world.

To further illustrate that we are more than overcomers in Christ Jesus, ***John 16:33(AMP)*** told us that *Jesus has deprived the world of its power to harm us.* Therefore, we are conquerors. Jesus won the war for us. He conquered Satan. So, every battle that we have, He will fight for us, if we turn it over to Him.

Sure, when we experience hurtful situations, the first fleshly thing we do is to walk away and/or blame God. We may even justify by bringing up the point that God did not protect us. I am reminded in **Romans 8:28** that the Lord said *that all things work together for the good of them that love Him and are the called according to His purpose.* That means we need to change any wrong attitudes that we have that tell us that God is not for us, or that He is not protecting us. Remember, God is timeless. Therefore, He doesn't operate in or by our timing, but by His own.

God gave His only son in **Romans 8:32** *for us. What good thing would He withhold from us* if we are seeking Him and serving Him? The problem is not on the giving end, but on the receiving end. It is not God. It is simply us with the problem. We, sometimes, do not know the power we possess. Our flesh and Satan are enmities against God. However, knowing our rights and privileges are keys to overcoming any obstacles or darts that Satan throws at us. Satan's motive is always to distract us from the position that we hold in Christ. Think of it like this. If Satan is doing his job to disrupt the kingdom of God, let us do our jobs even better by building the kingdom of God. Remember, we are agents of Christ who are seated at the right hand of the Father in the heavenly realms. God has raised Jesus above all principalities and powers. We, who were dead in trespasses, were raised in Christ Jesus. Therefore, poverty, sickness, and sin shall be trampled under our feet.

If we truly believe like this, why do we allow ourselves, as believers, to lack and die prematurely? Is it because no matter how much we profess it, we really do not know or believe in our authority in Christ? I am an overcomer. You are an overcomer. It is in Him that we live, move, and have our being. God has our lives in the palms of His hand. We must come to a point where we trust God so much, and know He has our best interest at heart, and His will is carried out in our lives. He will accomplish what He has set for our lives. Nothing catches God by surprise. What a great outcome for the believer! Our brother the Lord overcame the devil, and we can overcome too.

Overcomers simply overcome any situation they face because it is part of the inheritance. It is in our spiritual DNA. We are designed in the face of all adversity and oppositions to triumph because of the Father. Yes, hurt does hurt. But, we do not have to let it win. It is our choice. It is not just about what you are saying. More importantly, it is about who or what you believe. Will you believe the report of the Lord concerning your life and His love for you?

There was a period in my life when I was broken. I came close to a nervous breakdown. In 1986, Hurricane Hugo destroyed all that my husband and I possessed. We moved in with my parents, along with our three children. My parents were so loving and supportive during this difficult time. My husband's parents were deceased, so there was no assistance from his side of the family. I honestly was devastated over everything that we lost. Our jobs were lost, because of the devastation of this destructive storm.

One day, I was in our bedroom, and the room began to spin around and around. The bed felt like it was coming off the floor. In the natural, it was not really doing that, but I felt like I was losing my mind. My body appeared to be tossing from one side to the other. I felt a hand pulling me up by my nightgown. Scriptures began to flow into my mind: Greater is He that is in you, than he that is in the world! No weapon formed against you shall prosper! These were all overcoming scriptures. Suddenly, I thought to myself if God is saying this about me, what should I be saying? I began to open my mouth and scriptures began to flow. The Holy Spirit instructed me to get a pen and a piece of paper. I began to write what would be the first sermon I would preach. The Lord told me to entitle it, "Spiritual Warfare." ***Isaiah 59:19*** came to my mind, *"When the enemy shall come in, like a flood, the spirit of the Lord will lift a standard against him."* What do you think the standard is? Of course, it is the Word of God. If I had no Word in me at that time, the Holy Spirit would have been limited. Our Father operates through His Word. The Word reminds us; having done all there is to do, just stand.

I often hear people say that they are just holding on. The Bible did not say hold on. It says to stand. We can hold on to the end of a rope for a very long while. Eventually, because of the tiredness of our muscles, and perhaps the law of gravity, eventually we will let go. Perhaps, changing that image to feet that are firmly planted and grounded will be better suited as a confession of our posture and position we should take in Christ. Let us no longer be like the waves of the sea tossed back and forth. We do not have to move every time the wind takes a breath. To do so, means we are operating in a spirit of double-mindedness. We know that the Bible tells us that a double-minded, lukewarm individual will receive nothing from the Lord.

REPAIRER OF THE BREACH
Chapter 12

Satan does not want you to build up or raise up foundations and generations, because he does not want you to contribute to establishing God's kingdom. In fact, he wants you to help him to tear it down. Satan uses church hurt experiences to bring division among believers. He knows there is strength in unity, and he needs disunity to occur in order to concoct his manipulative plans. It is Satan's job to continue to war against the things and nature of God. It is time we stop letting him win. We, as Christians, need to take a stand and let go of any hurt, malice, or anger that we have toward others. Otherwise, it will continue to poison us with seeds of bitterness. We need to learn the true meaning of forgiveness, to heal individually and collectively as a Body of Blood-Washed Believers.

God chose, called, and put us on a journey that was designed specifically for us. When we accepted the gift of salvation, we agreed to a *Yes* from the Lord and a *Yes* to the Lord. Let us ask ourselves if we have broken that *Yes* agreement somewhere along the road because of our experiences with hurt. If the answer is yes, then we have breached the contract. God did not change His plans for us, no matter how it looks. But, we can change our plans for worse, if we choose to walk in disobedience, unforgiveness, and fleshly desires. **Romans 11:29** tells us that *the gifts and calling of the Lord are irrevocable*. Because of God's immutability, He cannot change His mind. **Malachi 3:6** says, *for I am God I cannot change*.

Hurt came to tempt us and to make us doubt the plan and will of God for our lives. Our purpose precedes our creation. Our purpose was laid out before we even came through our mother's womb. It was before the foundation of the Earth. Now, that is amazing! **Psalm 139:16** says, *His eyes saw our substance, while we were imperfect*. Therefore, our bodies belong to Him. It is not wise to lend our bodies as instruments of unrighteousness and sin. Although it may feel like the breach has been broken between God honoring His promises to you, I assure you that regardless of the circumstances, God still has a redemptive plan for your life. But, you must trust Him with your whole heart and being.

Isaiah 58:9-12 talks about the *restoration and repair aspect of a breach*. Because God has called us for a purpose before He created us, He equips us for fulfilling our purpose. To be honest, we really should be without excuses for not doing so. Everything pertaining to life and godliness have been written in the pages of the Bible. God calls us to do things that are in the given abilities that He has implanted within us. Sometimes, it takes a maturation process to fully realize all the potential He has placed within our being. Of course, Satan does not want this to happen. Therefore, he attacks with the sole purpose of creating hostility and division, particularly among the church. Allow Father God to restore and repair us. Then, and only then, can we go out and bring restoration to this hurting world. Throughout any ordeals that we may face in life, let our spirits remain strong, so that we do not break under pressure. Remember, there is no hurt or pain that our marvelous God cannot heal.

• • • • • • • • • •

A PRAYER FOR YOU

Father, in the name of Jesus, I thank you, because the prayers of the righteous have great power. I pray on behalf of all those who have experienced hurt or any kind of heartache. Thank you, for your loving grace and mercy that can set us all free. By the power vested in me, as a blood bought, born again believer whose prayers will not return void, I now release this prayer over them. Father, I am expecting change and breaking Satan's bondage over their lives. I declare and decree that they are coming forth from darkness into the light. You came that they might have life and have it more abundantly. Every demonic force sent to blind the eyes and hearts of these individuals, keeping them in darkness, I command the enemy to loose them and let them go in the Name of Jesus.

Lord, any hurts they experience will no longer be above your name. At the name of Jesus, I command every stronghold to break. I declare and decree, that you can and will fulfill the call that God has ordained for you. You will not quit, because it is part of your inheritance to triumph over all oppositions. Every negative word spoken over your life, I curse them at the root and command them to die and fall to the ground. For those words will not prosper. You shall live and not die and command the works of the Lord. In your path is life and there is no death. I pray that any curses be broken off your life, your family, and your ministry. Now, be resurrected through the power of Jesus Christ. Amen!

ACKNOWLEDGMENTS

I acknowledge my children, Dwayne, Dawn, and Shannon. Over the years since the passing of your father, you have been my support, my backbone; both emotionally and spiritually. Thank you for believing in me and my endeavors.

To the spiritual sons and daughters, I am elected to mentor, I value you! Your prayers and support gave me courage and strength to complete my first book. Please never stop praying; there is much more to learn and much more to write.

To my overseer, Mikel Brown, Pastor of Christian Joy Center Church, El Paso Texas, one Church in three locations, also founder of the Evangelical Christian Church Ministries (ECCM), affiliate churches, which I am proud and blessed to be a part. Pastor Brown, when you spoke to me about dealing with the root of hurt, I was encouraged. I received grace and strength to write from my heart. That began a liberation in me that I can't begin to articulate. I was wounded, I was damaged, and broken, but by God's grace, I can say today I am healed and I am free. Thank You.

I acknowledge Kingdom Builders Publications, LLC. In the beginning, I submitted a portion of my works to this company, and won a publishing, but had no idea how to start. This company were my eyes, hands, and mouth. They walked me through every process. Thanks for your labor of love to achieve a perfect work.

MORE ABOUT THE AUTHOR

Lavinia Young, 1954 – is the 5th of 14 children born in beautiful Gullah country; Beaufort, South Carolina. She and her family had humble beginnings, but they were always surrounded with care and reared with a very strong faith and family love.

Marriage yielded more than 30 years with LaVinia and her beloved Luke. One of her most precious and greatest accomplishments was being a wife, mother, and grandmother. Young has a ministry heart for the needs of people.

Her passion for outreach extends, but not limited to prisons, jails, and wherever God leads. Another accomplishment is her personal and pastoral ministry which spans over 35 years. This came with experience of servanthood, and collegiate studies. With tenacity, and a strong resolve, she graduated with full credentials from the Charis Bible College, Colorado Springs, Colorado.

She leads a thriving church in Metro-city, South Carolina where she now resides as the ordained senior pastor. Pastor Young founded Oasis of Hope Outreach Ministry of ECCM, out of a need to serve her community, and the Kingdom of God.

When she's not pastoring the flock, she can be found journaling, and spending time with her amazing family of three young adult children and eleven grandchildren. She loves corporate and private worship, cooking and traveling. She has traveled internationally, to Costa Rica, Central America, where she ministered divine healing to the masses.

Lavinia Young

www.ingramcontent.com/pod-product-compliance
Lightning Source LLC
Chambersburg PA
CBHW030529010526
44110CB00048B/967